SUPER CITIES!

INDIANAPOLIS

by Donna Griffin

arcadia®
CHILDREN'S BOOKS

Published by Arcadia Children's Books
A Division of Arcadia Publishing
Charleston, SC
www.arcadiapublishing.com

Super Cities is a trademark of Arcadia Publishing, Inc.

First published 2023

Manufactured in the United States of America.

ISBN 978-1-4671-9894-3

Library of Congress Control Number: 2022950473

Notice: The information in this book is true and complete to the best of our knowledge. It is offered without guarantee on the part of the author or Arcadia Publishing. The author and Arcadia Publishing disclaim all liability in connection with the use of this book.

Produced by Shoreline Publishing Group LLC
Santa Barbara, California
Designer: Patty Kelley
Production: Steve Solution

Contents

WELCOME TO Indianapolis!

Indianapolis, Indiana

Vroom, zoom, swish! Indianapolis, Indiana, is not only the state capital but the exact center of the Hoosier State! The city with the biggest population in the state, Indy leads the way in transportation, manufacturing, and technology.

The city is a sports fan's paradise. Indy has hosted more than 450 sporting events in the last 40 years, including US Olympic Trials, Super Bowl XLVI, NCAA Championships, and the Pan American Games, earning the nickname "Amateur Sports Capital of the World." And in the month of May, Indianapolis becomes the center of the sports world with the Indianapolis 500, one of the biggest single-day sporting events in the universe.

FAST FACTS
Indianapolis, Indiana
POPULATION: 887,642
FOUNDED: 1821
NICKNAMES:
**Crossroads of America,
Circle City, Indy, Naptown,
Capital City**

Indy's location earned it the nickname "Crossroads of America." Four interstate highways meet here. As America's 14th largest city, Indianapolis is all about Hoosier Hospitality and combines big-city connections with small-town charm.

When it comes to food, Farm-to-table is a way of life in Indy which is smack dab in the center of a state that is a leading producer of corn, soybeans, poultry, and popcorn. Local restaurants, farmers markets, festivals, and fairs put their own twist on down-home cooking, competing to have the freshest corn on the cob or the biggest pork tenderloin. Indianapolis is a great place to live . . . and to visit! Start your engines!

INDIANAPOLIS: Map It!

Indianapolis is the hub (that means the center) of a 10-county area of 1.6 million people called Central Indiana. That's where you'll find skyscrapers, big business, museums, and sports arenas only a short distance from farms, barns, and small towns with general stores and covered bridges. The White River runs through Indianapolis, along with the Central Canal, complete with a walking path and gondolas.

If you want to be in the center of the action, Monument Circle is the exact center of both Indianapolis and Indiana. Only a few miles away is the world's largest children's museum and the most famous race track in the world, the Indianapolis Motor Speedway.

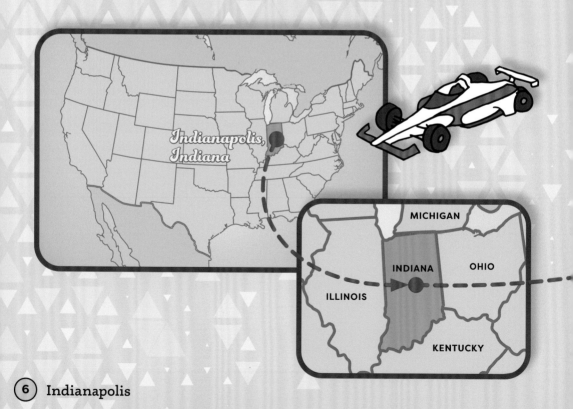

Indianapolis, Indiana

MICHIGAN

ILLINOIS

INDIANA

OHIO

KENTUCKY

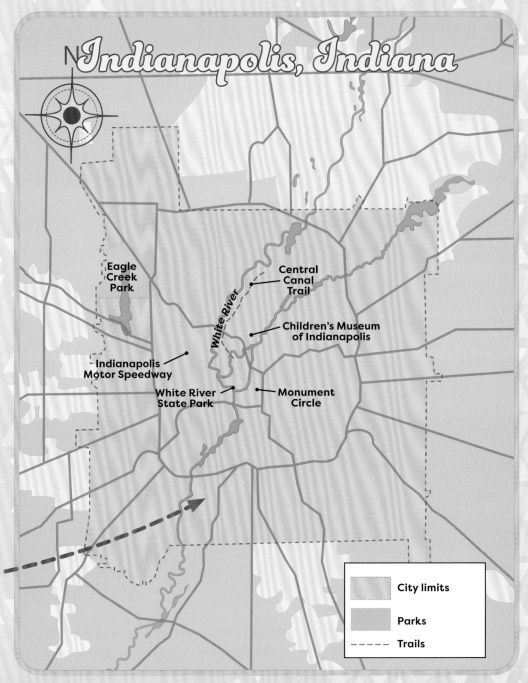

Indianapolis, Indiana

N

Eagle Creek Park

Central Canal Trail

White River

Children's Museum of Indianapolis

Indianapolis Motor Speedway

White River State Park

Monument Circle

City limits

Parks

----- Trails

Set the Scene

Here's what you'll see in this book . . . and in this fun and friendly city!

Hoosiers are proud of their downtown—and especially Monument Circle! At the center is the Soldiers and Sailors Monument, a beloved symbol of the city that is a must-see.

Located on 250 acres downtown, White River State Park is home to the Indianapolis Zoo, Indiana State Museum, NCAA Hall of Champions, and lots more. The park's canal is part of the Indianapolis Cultural Trail and includes a pathway for runners, bikers, and walkers.

Hoosiers take outdoor activities seriously with walking and biking trails throughout the city. Indy has an extensive park system that takes advantage of the woods, creeks, (we call them 'cricks' here) and green spaces dotting the area.

One of the country's largest city parks, Eagle Creek Park features more than 1,400 acres of water and 3,900 acres of forest for boating, swimming, fishing, and hiking. And yes, you can even spot a bald eagle there!

The Indiana State Capitol building in Indianapolis

The Indianapolis Motor Speedway is five miles west of Monument Circle. The speedway is an oval, however! It hosts the Indy 500 and other major auto races.

INDIANAPOLIS MEANS . . .

Indianapolis was designed to be the capital of Indiana, but the city's name came as an afterthought. In 1820 the state legislature of Indiana selected 10 commissioners, who chose a site for the state capital at the exact center of the state. But when the time came to name the new state capital, it took much discussion to fill in the blank. Some proposed "Tecumseh," for the chief of the area's Shawnee people. That and other names were all voted down. Then legislator Jeremiah Sullivan, who later became an Indiana Supreme Court Justice, proposed "Indianapolis." He combined *Indiana* and *polis*, (the Greek word for "city"). The new name was so popular it got votes from all ten commissioners!

Indiana state capitol dome

Naming Indiana

But how did Indiana get its name? The word itself means "Land of the Indians" or "Land of Indians." Following the division of the Northwest Territory in 1800, the name "Indiana" was chosen in recognition of the many Indigenous peoples—including the Miamis, Chippewa, Delawares, Shawnee, Iroquois, Mohegan, and others—who'd inhabited the land long before the arrival of European settlers.

Tecumseh

But before Indianapolis came to be, back in the late 1700s, the US created the Northwest Territory, which included land from what is now Ohio all the way up to northern Minnesota. In 1803, Ohio was carved out to become a state, followed by Indiana in 1816. Illinois changed from territory to state two years later. Michigan, Wisconsin, and Minnesota all became states out of the Northwest Territory soon, too.

unorganized territory organized as Northwest Territory

What Does It Mean To Be A Hoosier?

People don't agree on how the term "Hoosier" came about, but there's no doubt it is more than a nickname. For nearly 200 years, people from Indiana have been called "Hoosiers" (say HOO-zhers). It's such a part of the identity of Indiana, that the US government made it official in 2017. People there are not Indianans . . . they're Hoosiers.

Why are Hoosiers called Hoosiers?
Well, no one knows exactly how it happened and Hoosiers are okay with that. But historians, poets, and politicians have come up with several possible explanations:

➤ When a visitor hailed a pioneer cabin in Indiana or knocked upon its door, the settler would respond, "Who's yere?" And from this frequent response Indiana became the "Who's yere" or Hoosier state.

➤ Indiana rivermen were so successful in beating or "hushing" their enemies in fighting that they became known as "hushers," and eventually Hoosiers.

➤ A humorous explanation came from "The Hoosier Poet," James Whitcomb Riley. He said early Indiana settlers were fighters who scratched and bit off noses and ears. This became so common that a settler coming into a tavern the morning after a fight and seeing an ear on the floor would touch it with his toe and casually ask, "Whose ear?"

James Whitcomb Riley

Hoosier Hospitality: People in Indianapolis go the extra mile to be kind to visitors and make them feel welcome. Where else could Super Bowl fans be given hand-knit scarves?

Hoosier Hysteria: There's a reason one of the top sports movies of all time is called "Hoosiers." Hoosier Hysteria started with high school basketball when up to 15,000 screaming fans packed state high school championships in Hinkle Fieldhouse in Indianapolis (page 70). Hoosier fans are known for believing in their team, win or lose, and being very loud about it. Colts Nation (the fans) were named to the team's Ring of Honor. Both the Colts and Indiana Pacers homes are among the most feared by opponents.

MONUMENT CIRCLE

At the center of a circle at the center of the city at the center of the state stands a stone column that is 284 feet, six inches tall—the Soldiers and Sailors Monument.

Atop the column is the Victory statue, nicknamed Miss Indiana. It faces south as the official greeter of troops arriving back home.

Climb the column's 330 steps to get a 360-degree view of Indianapolis.

Finished in 1902, the monument was the first dedicated to common soldiers—"Silent Victors" of all the wars before World War I.

One of the figures on the base of the column shows an enslaved person freed of his chains. It was the first statue of an African American in the city when the monument went up in 1902.

FAST FACT

Indianapolis ranks first in the nation in the number of acres dedicated to honoring veterans, and second only to Washington D.C. in the number of monuments.

The Circle is the center of culture, celebration, history, and honor. Nightly light shows and all kinds of restaurants and music ring the monument which each holiday season becomes the Circle of Lights, or what Hoosiers call "the World's Largest Christmas Tree."

Hi, Fred: Mastodons, along with other large mammals, such as mammoths, giant bison, and saber-toothed cats roamed Indiana during the Ice Age, about 13,000 years ago. "Fred" is a mastodon skeleton discovered on a farm near Fort Wayne and is now on display at the Indiana State Museum.

The Mound Builders

Angel Mounds is the site of one of the largest settlements of early people, who lived in Indiana near present-day Evansville on the Ohio River. Some earthworks were made between 200 BCE and 200 CE by two distinct cultures of people. Other people lived there until the 1400s. Archaeologists have found many artifacts, including stone tools, pottery, and a carved stone figurine.

Life for Locals: In the earliest days of what is now Indiana, Indigenous peoples lived on land thick with forest and with a variety of animal life and rivers full of fish. Eventually, these groups grew crops. They lived and traveled along the many rivers that provided transportation as well as food and water. The Miami and Delaware people lived near what is now Indianapolis.

Crossroads: Even centuries ago, this land was a crossroads. At first the Miami people called it Myaamionki, the place of the Miami, since it was their territorial home. But because there were many other indigenous peoples living and traveling across the land, they called it Mihtohseenionki, the Peoples' Place.

Free Trade Zone: Kekionga was a center of trade on the Maumee River in what is now Fort Wayne, Indiana. The Miami people established Kekionga as a free trade zone, where friends and enemies exchanged goods in safety. Located at the land bridge between the Maumee and Wabash rivers, it connected trade routes east to the Atlantic Ocean and south to the Gulf of Mexico.

Drawing of Kekionga from 1790.

VIEW OF THE MAUMEE TOWNS
DESTROYED BY GENERAL HARMAR
October, 1790

SHAWANEES   DELAWARES

Here Come the French: French explorers were the first Europeans to arrive in the area. On Dec. 3, 1679, Robert LaSalle was the first white man to visit what would become Indiana.

Robert LaSalle

Culture Clash: The French and Indigenous peoples managed to live fairly peacefully for a century or so. But when British colonists came to the Ohio River Valley in the 1700s, they wanted the Miami and Delaware people to adopt their culture and live like them—or leave.

Here Come the Americans: During the American Revolution (1775-1783), General George Rogers Clark of the American army led a surprise attack on the British Fort Sackville at Vincennes, Indiana. When the American Revolution ended in 1783 with The Treaty of Paris, the United States gained the Northwest Territory, which was of the land west of the Appalachian Mountains, including what would become Indiana.

George Rogers Clark

A Step Against Slavery: In 1787, the United States Constitution did not address slavery, but the Northwest Ordinance (right) did. That set of laws governed the Northwest Territory, and included freedom of religion, right to trial by jury, and public education. Slavery was illegal in the Territory.

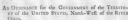

Gen. Clark accepts surrender of the British at Vincennes.

1800: Indiana's path to statehood took 16 years, beginning in 1800 with the appointment of Territorial Governor William Henry Harrison. Vincennes, located on the Wabash River, was named the territorial capital. Established in 1732 as a French fur trading and military post, Vincennes is the oldest city in Indiana.

Indiana Grows: William Henry Harrison was the first governor of the Indiana Territory in 1800. He added nearly 3 million acres of land through battles against or treaties with indigenous peoples. The most famous was the 1811 "Battle of Tippecanoe" in Indiana. Fame from that battle helped him get elected president in 1840. However, Harrison caught pneumonia at his inaugural parade and died one month later on April 4, 1841. It was the shortest term of any US president, and he was the first to die in office.

William Henry Harrison

FAST FACT

William Henry Harrison's grandson, Benjamin Harrison, became the 23rd President of the United States. They are the only grandfather and grandson to serve as president.

Benjamin Harrison

It's a State! The first state election was held on Aug. 5, 1816. Jonathan Jennings was elected governor. In November 1816, the first General Assembly met and approved the State's Constitution. One month later, President James Madison admitted Indiana to the Union as the 19th state, on December 11, 1816.

SEAL OF THE STATE OF INDIANA 1816

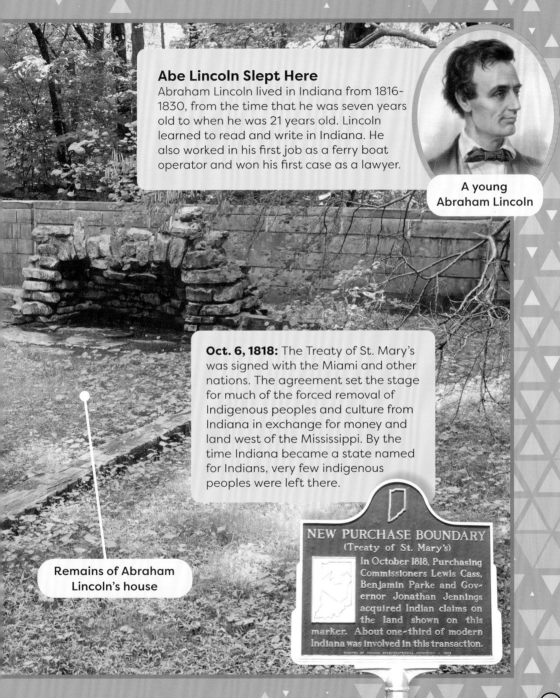

Abe Lincoln Slept Here

Abraham Lincoln lived in Indiana from 1816–1830, from the time that he was seven years old to when he was 21 years old. Lincoln learned to read and write in Indiana. He also worked in his first job as a ferry boat operator and won his first case as a lawyer.

A young Abraham Lincoln

Oct. 6, 1818: The Treaty of St. Mary's was signed with the Miami and other nations. The agreement set the stage for much of the forced removal of Indigenous peoples and culture from Indiana in exchange for money and land west of the Mississippi. By the time Indiana became a state named for Indians, very few indigenous peoples were left there.

Remains of Abraham Lincoln's house

NEW PURCHASE BOUNDARY
(Treaty of St. Mary's)

In October 1818, Purchasing Commissioners Lewis Cass, Benjamin Parke and Governor Jonathan Jennings acquired Indian claims on the land shown on this marker. About one-third of modern Indiana was involved in this transaction.

ERECTED BY INDIANA SESQUICENTENNIAL COMMISSION · 1966

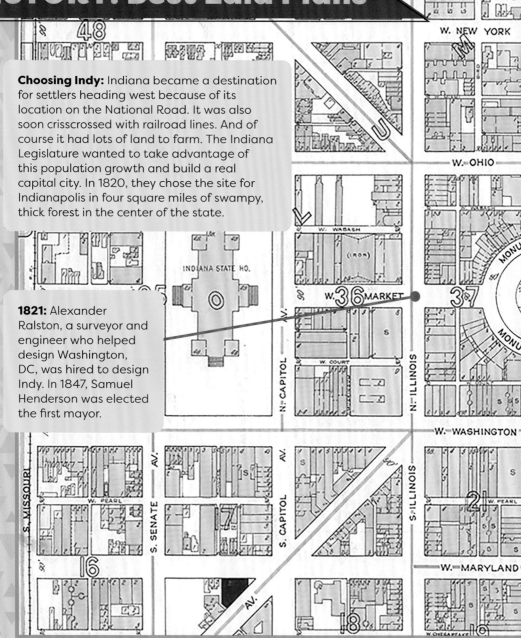

Choosing Indy: Indiana became a destination for settlers heading west because of its location on the National Road. It was also soon crisscrossed with railroad lines. And of course it had lots of land to farm. The Indiana Legislature wanted to take advantage of this population growth and build a real capital city. In 1820, they chose the site for Indianapolis in four square miles of swampy, thick forest in the center of the state.

1821: Alexander Ralston, a surveyor and engineer who helped design Washington, DC, was hired to design Indy. In 1847, Samuel Henderson was elected the first mayor.

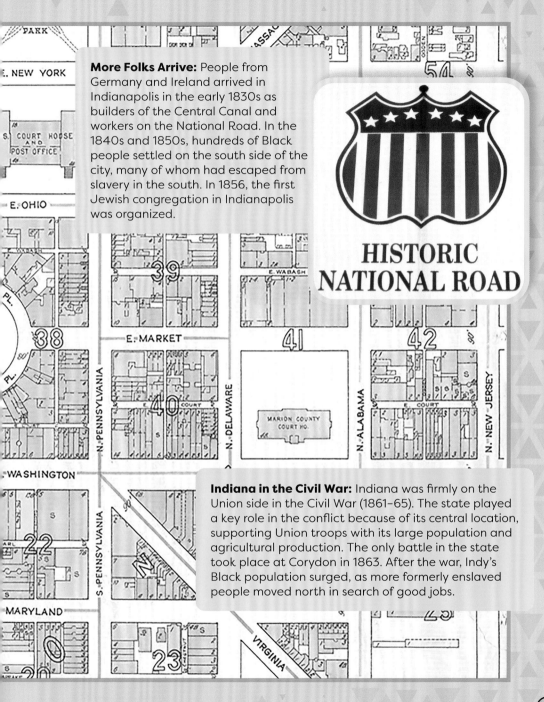

More Folks Arrive: People from Germany and Ireland arrived in Indianapolis in the early 1830s as builders of the Central Canal and workers on the National Road. In the 1840s and 1850s, hundreds of Black people settled on the south side of the city, many of whom had escaped from slavery in the south. In 1856, the first Jewish congregation in Indianapolis was organized.

HISTORIC NATIONAL ROAD

Indiana in the Civil War: Indiana was firmly on the Union side in the Civil War (1861–65). The state played a key role in the conflict because of its central location, supporting Union troops with its large population and agricultural production. The only battle in the state took place at Corydon in 1863. After the war, Indy's Black population surged, as more formerly enslaved people moved north in search of good jobs.

HISTORY: No Mean City

The first half of the 20th century brought big changes to Indianapolis, which was quickly becoming a leader in agriculture, manufacturing, and transportation. The city was among the first with paved streets and, in 1881, with electric street lights. Thanks to its location as a railroad center, Indianapolis had developed an economy that included flour mills, pork packing, blacksmiths, and machine shops.

FAST FACT

Indianapolis boomed in population. Between 1850 and 1900, the city's population exploded nearly 2,000 percent—from 8,091 to 169,164.

1900: On January 1, 1900, Indy opened an electric railcar called the interurban. These railcars operated on streets between Indy and communities within 120 miles of Indianapolis. By 1920, the streetcar system had a ridership of 126 million. It operated until the 1950s.

1902: The most important structure in Indianapolis was created in Circle Park beginning in 1888. After years of discussion, the state of Indiana decided to build a monument to veterans of the Civil War. Dedicated in May 1902 to "all soldiers and sailors of wars," the Soldiers and Sailors Monument replaced Circle Park and became Monument Circle.

What Does "Mean" Mean? Since Indy was literally built from scratch, it took longer for government, businesses, and factories to be built. But one of the first buildings was Indianapolis City Hall. It opened in 1910. Its cornerstone reads, "I am myself a citizen of no mean city." What do they mean "mean?" Well, they didn't mean "not nice." In this case *mean* means average. That is, "we're an above-average city!"

Vroom, Vroom: Indianapolis was an early center for car making and design. In 1905, local car salesman Carl Fisher and three partners built a track for testing and private races between car makers. The 2.5-mile track west of the city became the Indianapolis Motor Speedway, where the first Indy 500 was run in 1911.

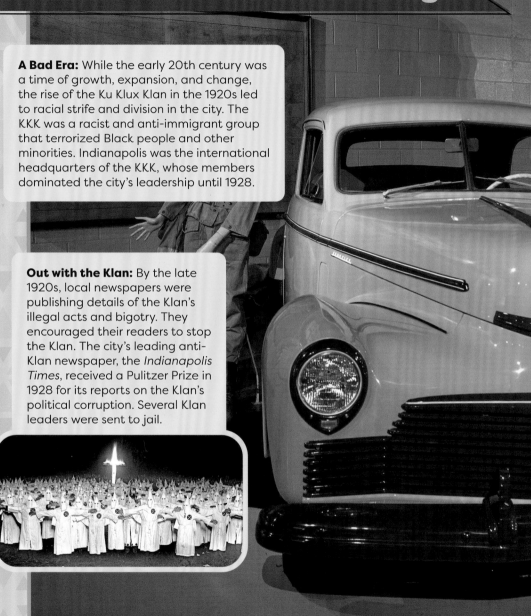

A Bad Era: While the early 20th century was a time of growth, expansion, and change, the rise of the Ku Klux Klan in the 1920s led to racial strife and division in the city. The K.K.K. was a racist and anti-immigrant group that terrorized Black people and other minorities. Indianapolis was the international headquarters of the K.K.K., whose members dominated the city's leadership until 1928.

Out with the Klan: By the late 1920s, local newspapers were publishing details of the Klan's illegal acts and bigotry. They encouraged their readers to stop the Klan. The city's leading anti-Klan newspaper, the *Indianapolis Times*, received a Pulitzer Prize in 1928 for its reports on the Klan's political corruption. Several Klan leaders were sent to jail.

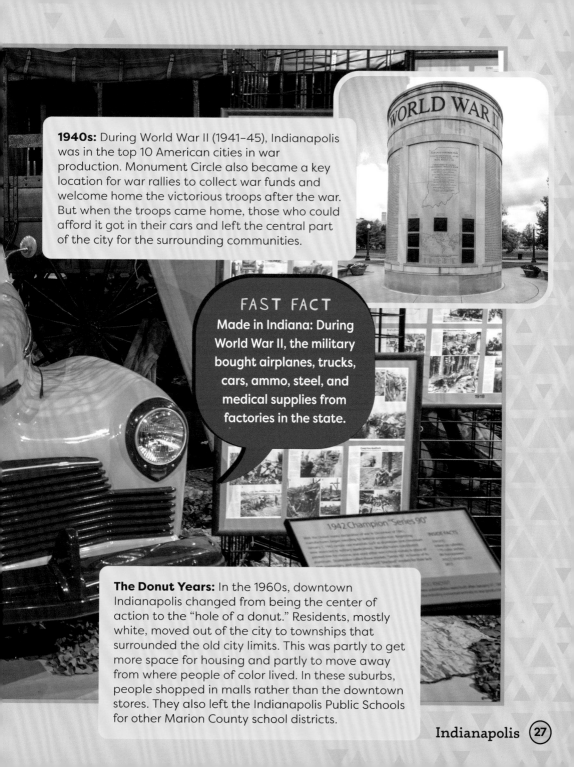

1940s: During World War II (1941–45), Indianapolis was in the top 10 American cities in war production. Monument Circle also became a key location for war rallies to collect war funds and welcome home the victorious troops after the war. But when the troops came home, those who could afford it got in their cars and left the central part of the city for the surrounding communities.

FAST FACT
Made in Indiana: During World War II, the military bought airplanes, trucks, cars, ammo, steel, and medical supplies from factories in the state.

The Donut Years: In the 1960s, downtown Indianapolis changed from being the center of action to the "hole of a donut." Residents, mostly white, moved out of the city to townships that surrounded the old city limits. This was partly to get more space for housing and partly to move away from where people of color lived. In these suburbs, people shopped in malls rather than the downtown stores. They also left the Indianapolis Public Schools for other Marion County school districts.

Indianapolis

A New Government: In 1969, the city and surrounding Marion County combined to form UnivGov (short for Unified Government), to help grow the city's population and economy. It was not a perfect plan, however, and came at a cost to disadvantaged groups while mainly benefitting wealthier white communities.

Busing: In the 1970s, the federal government sued Indianapolis to better integrate its schools. The "white flight" of earlier decades had created schools that were pretty much all white (outer areas) or all Black (closer to center of city). A court ruling forced the school district to transfer (on daily buses) students in either direction, mostly taking Black students to white schools. The plan was controversial and often created even more problems. Indiana still had very non-diverse schools; the busing continued until 2016!

We Want Sports: In 1979, Mayor William H. Hudnut III helped create the Indiana Sports Corporation to attract sports events, teams, and organizational headquarters to Indianapolis. The plan worked. The city hosted the 1982 National Sports Festival, the 1987 Pan American Games, and built new pro football and basketball stadiums. The NCAA moved to Indy in 1999 as well.

Here Come the Colts: In a daring gamble in 1982, Hudnut organized construction of the Hoosier Dome, a 61,000-seat stadium. One problem: At the time, Indy did not *have* an NFL team! But two years later, the city convinced the Colts to sneak out of Baltimore (literally! They moved at night!) and move to the Hoosier Dome. As the Indanapolis Colts, they won the Super Bowl in 2007.

The Hoosier Dome was the home of the Colts; it was torn down in 2008.

2021 NCAA FINA

INDY TODAY

As Indy entered its third century, the city came full circle as a national and global leader in manufacturing, technology, and distribution.

Technology: Indianapolis is known for emerging technologies such as advanced technology vehicles, biofuels, renewable energy, sustainable power, and energy efficiency. Indianapolis has been ranked one of the best cities to start a business as well as one of the best cities for women in tech with major global companies like Salesforce and Infosys.

Medical: Indianapolis is one of the leading manufacturing cities in the US and home to global medical companies like Eli Lilly and Company, Roche Diagnostics, and Zimmer Biomet.

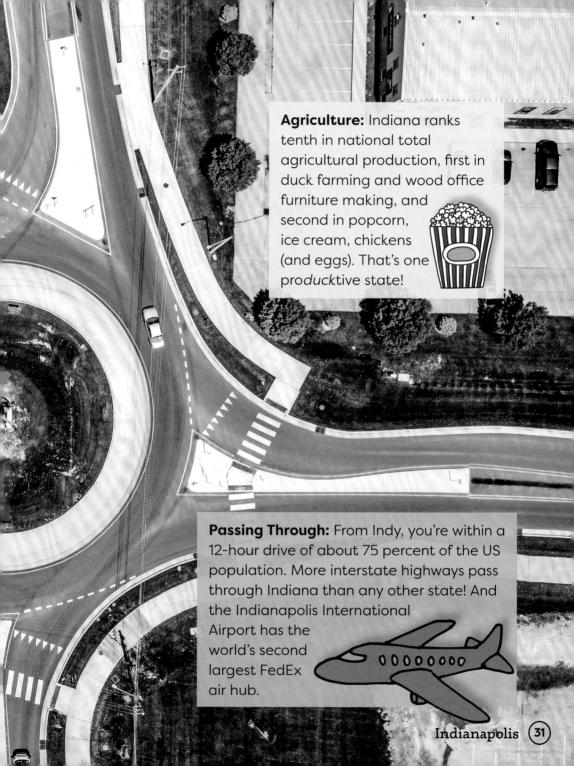

Agriculture: Indiana ranks tenth in national total agricultural production, first in duck farming and wood office furniture making, and second in popcorn, ice cream, chickens (and eggs). That's one pro*duck*tive state!

Passing Through: From Indy, you're within a 12-hour drive of about 75 percent of the US population. More interstate highways pass through Indiana than any other state! And the Indianapolis International Airport has the world's second largest FedEx air hub.

People from the Past!

Meet some interesting people from Indianapolis's past.

Col. Eli Lilly (1838–1898)

After serving in the Civil War, Lilly founded his chemical company, named for him, in 1876. It became one of the nation's biggest makers of prescription drugs and medicines. Lilly's success helped make him a leader in his home city. He led the way to creating the Chamber of Commerce and contributed a lot to the Charity Organization Society to help people in need. The company is still a big deal today, and Lilly Endowment Inc. is one of America's biggest foundations, giving millions of dollars each year to people and organizations.

Richard G. Lugar (1932–2019)

Richard G. Lugar was first elected mayor of Indianapolis in 1967, during a challenging time for the city. During those four years, he transformed the government, combining it with the larger county. In 1971, he became the first elected mayor of the combined city-county government. Lugar went on to become one of Indiana's United States senators from 1977 to 2013, where he specialized in foreign relations.

Madam C.J. Walker (1867–1919)

In the early 1900s, Madam C.J. Walker became the first self-made Black woman millionaire. She created a hair-care products company and made real estate investments. She is one of only 15 women inducted into the National Business Hall of Fame. She fought for the rights of African Americans and supported local musicians and artists with the construction of the Madam Walker Theatre in 1927. The theater remains the centerpiece of Black culture and history in Indianapolis and is on the National Register of Historic Places.

William H. Hudnut III (1932–2016)

William "Bill" Hudnut served as mayor of Indianapolis for four terms, from 1976 to 1991, the only mayor to serve for more than two terms. He was a leader in spreading the fame of the city. During his term, Indy became a sports capital by hosting national and international sports events. Hudnut is most known for leading the work to build the Hoosier Dome, convincing the Colts to move to Indy. He also oversaw building the Circle Centre Mall. In 1990, Hudnut issued a proclamation welcoming gay and lesbian visitors to a celebration on the Circle, signaling the city's openness.

Indianapolis Cultural Trail

Discover some of Indy's coolest and most historic areas on the eight-mile Indianapolis Cultural Trail. It gives families a chance to explore the city in an up-close, outdoor way. Good news: the trail and its activities are free!

Start downtown with picnic areas, a splash pad, and the Colts Canal Playspace, the largest downtown playground.

Walk or bike to surrounding neighborhoods for all kinds of restaurants and entertainment activities.

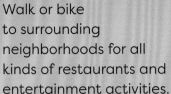

One popular spot is the Canal Walk in White River State Park. You can bring your own bike or use the Indiana Pacers Bikeshare stations.

Enjoy the local art, murals, and sculptures on the path, too.

The Cultural Trail connects people who shaped the city. Celebrate with festivities such as the Italian Street Festival, Greek Festival, Irish Fest, and German Fest. Each year the city also hosts the International Festival and Fiesta Indianapolis to celebrate Hispanic culture.

Black Lives Matter in Indy

While Black people have been leaders in business, government, and culture in Indianapolis since its beginning, they were usually segregated (separated) from white people until the late 1960s. Tensions stemming from Indy's history still exist, but the city has seen positive change. Today, almost 30 percent of Indy's population is Black.

Thanks, Madam!

In 1910, Madam C.J. Walker (page 33) moved her business to Indianapolis. Her store on Indiana Avenue became the heart of the African American community until the 1950s. Today the Madam Walker Legacy Center celebrates not only Walker's business success but the thriving Black culture in the city.

Beating Racism on the Court

Crispus Attucks High School opened in Indianapolis in 1927 as the city's only secondary school for Black students. Many of the faculty came from teaching at Black colleges in the South. That school gained fame for its athletic and academic programs in spite of being banned from competing against white schools in the city until 1941. In 1955, Attucks captured the state boys basketball championship. Led by future NBA Hall of Fame player Oscar Robertson, the team repeated its victory in 1956. The school is still open, serving students of all backgrounds.

Oscar Robertson

Landmark for Peace

On April 4, 1968, the United States was in the midst of the Civil Rights Movement when presidential candidate Sen. Robert Kennedy came to Indianapolis for a speech. That night, Martin Luther King Jr. was killed by a white gunman in Memphis. Hours later, Kennedy spoke about King and the tragedy of his death. The words from that speech in Indianapolis are engraved at Kennedy's gravesite in Washington D.C. The park where Kennedy spoke is now Dr. Martin Luther King Jr. Park and is home to the Landmark for Peace Memorial.

FAST FACT

In 1968 Julia Carson worked for an Indianapolis congressman and saw Robert Kennedy speak. In 1997, Carson became the first woman and first African American to represent Indianapolis in the US Congress, serving until her death in 2007. Her grandson, André Carson, was elected to replace her in 2008.

Indiana Black Expo

The Indiana Black Expo (IBE) began in 1970 to host community events and positive programs that support the lives of African American families. Its Summer Celebration includes concerts, a film festival, church services, business and education conferences, free health screenings, and other cultural events.

Julia Carson

Indy's Crazy Weather

If you don't like the weather in Indiana, just stick around, it will change. The official climate may say four seasons—including warm, humid summers, and cold, snowy short winters—but Hoosiers know different. Indianapolis is caught in the middle of southerly winds from the Gulf region that bring warm, wet air into the state. This humid air collides with polar air brought southward by the jet stream from Canada. This makes for extremes and unpredictability in weather—floods, ice storms, blizzards, and tornadoes—Hoosiers have seen it all. The best time of year to visit Indianapolis for warm-weather activities is from mid-June to late September—unless Mother Nature's weather signals get crossed.

Crazy Weather Facts

Highest Temperature ever recorded: 106 on July 14, 1936
Lowest Temperature ever recorded: -27 on January 19, 1994
Maximum rain in 24 hours: 7.20 inches on September 1, 2003
Maximum snow in 1 season: 58.2 inches in 1981-82
Earliest Date of First Measurable Snowfall: October 18, 1989
Latest Date of Last Measurable Snowfall: May 9, 1923

Spring

Summer

Fall

Winter

Wild Weather Stories!

Over the years, Indianapolis has been the site of over-the-top storms.

April 3, 1974: Super Outbreak

On April 3 and 4, 1974, Indiana experienced the most devastating tornado outbreak (when multiple tornadoes happen in a short period of time) in its history. In six hours, 21 tornadoes struck 38 counties, killing 47 people and injuring nearly 900, with property losses for nearly 6,000 families. At least four more tornadoes swept through Central Indiana during the evening between Indianapolis, Lafayette, and Fort Wayne.

Get Out of the Way!

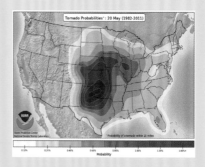

Indiana is in Tornado Alley, a part of the US that stretches across the Great Plains and is known for tornadoes. Preparing and keeping an eye out for tornadoes is a part of living in Central Indiana. While tornadoes usually occur in spring, in Indiana, they can happen anytime. Most aren't that strong, but they can still do damage. Others, however, can be devastating. The Super Outbreak led the National Weather Service to develop better radar and satellites to track tornadoes and warn people when they may be coming. Hoosiers know to listen to such warnings!

Blizzard of 1978

People in Indiana still remember the Blizzard of 1978 each January 25–27. Back then, most people did not believe the first-ever blizzard warning for the entire state. Snow fell in the Indianapolis area for about 34 hours. The storm set records for the most snow in one month: 30.6 inches. At one point, there were 20 inches of snow on the ground in the city! Indy was basically shut down for three days. The snow emergency meant that roads were closed! Doctors and emergency personnel were forced to reach people on skis and snowmobiles. Seventy people died during the storm.

FAST FACT
Since the Blizzard of 1978, Indianapolis made better plans to deal with so much snow, buying snow removal gear and snow plows!

Famous People Today

Jane Pauley, Newscaster

Jane Pauley is best known for her many years on "The Today Show" and "Dateline NBC." She has been on "CBS Sunday Morning" since 2016, the only female anchor on a Sunday morning news program. In 2009, she gave money to help build Jane Pauley Community Health Clinics in her East Side Indy neighborhood and throughout Central Indiana. Pauley is a powerful advocate in the field of mental health after being diagnosed with mental illness at the age of 50. A graduate of Indiana University, Pauley has been married since 1980 to *Doonesbury* cartoonist Garry Trudeau.

Ryan Murphy, TV Show Creator

Born in Indianapolis in 1965, Murphy is a screenwriter, director, and producer. He's best known for creating a number of hit television series, including "Glee" and "American Horror Story." He has won several Emmys, a Tony Award, and Golden Globe Award. His 2020 play "The Prom," tells the story of stage stars from New York who try to pump up their images by standing up for a gay high schooler in Indiana who is barred from attending her prom. Murphy used the play to reflect on his struggles of growing up gay in Indiana.

Kenneth 'Babyface' Edmonds, Musician

Born in 1959 in Indianapolis, Edmonds has written and produced more than 25 number-one R&B hits and has won many Grammy Awards. In 1989, he co-founded LaFace Records with L.A. Reid. Since then, Edmonds has worked with many of the top musical acts in the world, including Whitney Houston and Boyz II Men. He returned home in 2022 to receive a Walk of Fame star at the Madam Walker Legacy Center.

David Letterman, Comedian and TV Host

Born in Indianapolis in 1947, David Letterman got his start here as a TV weatherman. Letterman went on to a 33-year career as America's longest running late-night television host on "Late Night with David Letterman." Viewers across the world tuned in for his unique Hoosier-born humor. Letterman has never forgotten his Indy roots. A graduate of Ball State University in Muncie, he funded the campus radio station, scholarships, and a lecture/workshop series. The university named its communication building after him.

Things to see in Indianapolis

Indoors and outside, Indianapolis is packed with great things for you and your family to explore.

Children's Museum of Indianapolis

This place calls itself the "World's Largest Children's Museum!" And it's all about hands-on exploring. It has one of the largest collections of fossils in its Dinosphere area, where you can touch real dinosaur fossils and talk with archaeologists as they work.

There is something to do everywhere you turn. In an exhibit about Ancient Greece, find out about about Greek foods, music and dances, and learn about conservation efforts for sea turtles on the 8,000-mile Greek coast. Elsewhere in the museum, discover how four 20th-century children changed the world. Experience what it's like to be an astronaut and see treasures uncovered from the sea, including from a real shipwreck in the Caribbean.

Be sure to get outside to run, drive, jump, putt, and play a variety of sports while learning about Indiana sports legends in the Riley Children's Health Sports Legends Experience. And the amazing, 43-foot glass sculpture "Fireworks of Glass" is by famous artist Dale Chihuly!

Things to See in Indianapolis

Conner Prairie

History comes alive and you can be a part of it at Conner Prairie. The museum offers historically themed, indoor and outdoor areas on 800 acres of wooded property. It's in Fishers, a northeast suburb of Indy. In the 1836 Prairietown exhibit, kids can step back in time and join in daily routines from many years ago. You can also live like a Lenape person, go on an 1863 Civil War Journey, visit the Tree Outpost, or soar above Conner Prairie in a helium-filled, tethered balloon.

White River State Park

White River State Park is America's only state park that combines museums, public art, entertainment, sports, and green spaces in more than 250 acres. Explore the park by bike, Segway, or your own two feet and visit the Indianapolis Zoo, Eiteljorg Museum of American Indians and Western Art, NCAA Hall of Champions, Indiana State Museum, and Victory Field.

Indiana State Museum

The Indiana State Museum is really packed with several days worth of fun and exploration.

➤ Feel the fang of a saber-toothed cat, explore a subglacial ice tunnel, and wind your way through replicas of caves that house the bones of many now-extinct animals.

➤ Touch artifacts and specimens like rocks and minerals, animals and plants. Use the tools of a naturalist and engage with on-staff scientists and historical Hoosiers, as well as other experts in the state, to discover the world around you.

➤ View artifacts from the museum's archaeology collection including a Clovis arrow point from 10,000 years ago, 2,000-year-old ceramic pottery, jewelry, and more.

FAST FACT
The museum also has a 3-story IMAX movie theater.

NCAA Hall of Champions

Test your sports knowledge and be inspired at The NCAA Hall of Champions. All 24 NCAA sports are included, with current team rankings, video highlights, and items donated from colleges around the nation. The most popular place is on the second level, where you can play a quick basketball game in the retro 1930s gym and then compete virtually and test your skills through sports simulators.

Things to See in Indianapolis

Eiteljorg Museum

The Eiteljorg is a great place to learn about the first peoples in Indiana, including the Miami, sharing stories of young people who live and celebrate their Miami heritage in the 21st Century. There are also displays of painting and sculpture from the American West, as well as artifacts and artwork from other Indigenous peoples from North America.

Bang those Drums!

The Rhythm Discovery Center is the world's top drum and percussion museum. Where else can you strike a giant gong, slap the bongos, and sit at a Beatles drum that Ringo Starr used to record the group's hits? Bring your ear plugs and try hands-on percussion instruments from around the world, and then take a seat at the drums in a soundproof room where you can create your own beat.

Indianapolis Motor Speedway Hall of Fame and Museum

The IMS museum celebrates the need for speed! You can see the actual cars that won the Indy 500 and the trophies they earned. The best part is the tour of the track. You board a bus for a trip around the world's most famous race track and even get out at the start/finish line for your own "Kiss the Bricks" photo moment.

FAST FACT

Many of the place names in Indiana come from the history and culture of the area's early peoples. For example, the White River gets its name from the Miami word "waapikaminki" which means "on the white water."

Museums— Go See 'Em!

Medical History Museum

The Indiana Medical History Museum is in an 1896 building on the grounds of the former Central State Hospital for the Insane. Exhibits show how medicine has changed over the years, especially how doctors treat people with mental illnesses. You can also see some of the old-time doctors' instruments and medicines. You'll be happy to see how far we've come since those early days!

James Whitcomb Riley Museum

The James Whitcomb Riley Museum Home is located in the heart of the historic Lockerbie Square. Riley, a famous Hoosier poet, lived there late in his life. The Museum Home opened in 1922 to show the history of James Whitcomb Riley and his Victorian world. The Home features the same furnishings and fancy decorations that Riley enjoyed during his lifetime. See the desk where he wrote some of his most well-known poems, such as "Little Orphant Annie" and "The Raggedy Man."

James Whitcomb Riley

Kurt Vonnegut Museum

Kurt Vonnegut was one of Indianapolis's most famous writers. His novels combined science fiction, humor, and some beautiful writing about being a human being. At this museum, you can see a typewriter he used, next to his famous red rooster lamp. Then look over the rejection letters Vonnegut received from editors during his career.

Kurt Vonnegut

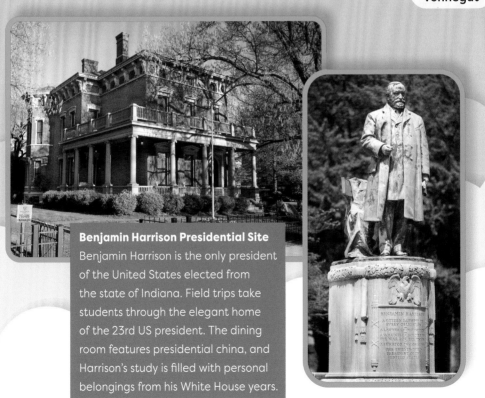

Benjamin Harrison Presidential Site

Benjamin Harrison is the only president of the United States elected from the state of Indiana. Field trips take students through the elegant home of the 23rd US president. The dining room features presidential china, and Harrison's study is filled with personal belongings from his White House years.

IT'S OFFICIAL!

CITY SYMBOL:
The city's only official symbol is the flag, which represents Monument Circle and the Indianapolis motto, Crossroads of America.

STATE INSECT:
Say's firefly

SAY WHAT?

Indiana's most recent state symbol came when a group of school kids refused to stop "bugging" the government to name a state insect. They worked for three years to have the Say's firefly named as official state insect—and they got their wish in 2018. Before that, Indiana was one of only three states that did not have a state insect. Not only is this species of firefly native to Indiana, it also is named after a Hoosier—Thomas Say. The scientist was considered the Father of North American Entomology (study of insects).

STONE:
Salem limestone

BIRD:
Cardinal

**OFFICIAL
INDIANA
STATE STUFF**

SONG:
"On the Banks of the
Wabash, Far Away,"
by Paul Dresser

FLOWER:
Peony

TREE:
Tulip tree

RIVER:
Wabash River

Indianapolis 53

Indiana State Fair

For more than 150 summers, the Indiana State Fair in Indianapolis has showcased youth and agriculture. As the sixth-oldest state fair in America, the Indiana State Fair attracts more than 800,000 people each year. The current Indiana State Fairgrounds & Event Center location opened in 1892 after the first 40 Indiana State Fairs were held at various sites around the state.

When it comes to a Taste of the Fair, there is every deep-fried food imaginable, and those that no one ever thought about. In a typical three weeks at the fair, the Dairy Bar sells more than 62,000 milkshakes and 32,000 grilled cheese sandwiches.

Midway rides are just one part of the fair's activities that include hot air balloons, tractor pulls, cheerleading, harness racing, baton twirling, sheep shearing, and championship rodeo competitions.

Exhibits on auto racing, agriculture, and technology give fairgoers the chance to see what changes are ahead for Hoosiers.

FAST FACT
More than 6,000 exhibitors from across the state show nearly 46,000 animals— pigs, goats, horses, ponies, llamas, and alpacas.

Indianapolis

Eating Indy Style!

Farmers Markets: With Indiana a leader in farming and agriculture, farmer's markets are in nearly every city. Most Hoosiers agree there's nothing like picking up fresh-off-the-farm fruits and vegetables from a market or a roadside stand. The Original Farmers' Market is held in front of City Market and is one of central Indiana's longest-running and largest farmers' markets.

Pork Tenderloins: You have to see Indy's top food to believe it and then the hard part comes—eating it! Plenty of restaurants serve this giant disc of pork, pounded thin, breaded, fried, placed between a comically small bun, and topped with lettuce, tomato, and maybe a couple of pickles. Up for the challenge?

Soul Food: Hoosiers love comfort food that crosses cultures, like ribs, fried chicken, wings, catfish, macaroni and cheese, and collard greens, and don't forget the chicken and waffles!

Donuts and Sweet Treats: Donuts are a delight in Indy. The most popular places usually have long lines and sell out before noon. Hoosiers like glazed yeast donuts, especially when they practically melt in your mouth. But donuts in all flavors and combinations are a sweet treat anytime in Indy. Also, Indiana's unofficial favorite pie is sugar cream pie.

Ice Cream: In most places, the drive-in diners of the 1950s are long gone—but not in Indiana. Most smalltown and city neighborhoods have an ice cream shop like the one that Hoosier native John Mellencamp sang about in a famous pop song. Whether it's eating in the car or running around in the picnic area, the hamburgers, hot dogs, and fries paired with ice cream shakes, cups, and cones are old-fashioned treats.

Big Mouth

Indy's competitive spirit shows up in eating, too. Professional fast eater Joey Chesnut has set several world records in Indianapolis. He ate just over 17 pounds of shrimp cocktails in ten minutes at St. Elmo restaurant in downtown Indy in 2018. In 2022, he powered through 32 24-ounce servings of popcorn during an Indianapolis Indians game.

Art for All

Newfields: Newfields connects art and nature through 152-acres of galleries, gardens, a historic home, performance spaces, a nature preserve, and sculpture park. The centerpiece of Newfields is the Indianapolis Museum of Art, among the 10 largest and oldest general art museums in the nation. Artists from around the world are featured in the museum.

FAST FACT
Robert Indiana (1928–2018) was born in New Castle, Indiana, and grew up in Indianapolis. See his original *LOVE* sculpture (1970) at the Indianapolis Museum of Art.

Bigger Than Life: Much of Indy's outdoor art can be seen downtown along the Cultural Trail or in the nearby neighborhoods of Broad Ripple, Fountain Square, and Mass Ave. In 2012, 34 artists created 46 murals to celebrate Indy's hosting of Super Bowl XLVI, including one of Indy native Kurt Vonnegut on Mass Ave.

FAST FACT

The Indy Arts Council has identified 3,090 works of art in Marion County in its first-of-a-kind Public Art For All Census. You can find an interactive map and days for walking tours on the Indy Arts website.

Major Mural: A five-story mural downtown honors bike racer Marshall "Major" Taylor. In 1901, he was the first African American to win a world championship in a sport. The mural is the first of the Bicentennial Legends series, celebrating Indianapolis becoming a city. It's near the site of the bike shop where a 12-year-old Taylor earned his famous nickname by performing cycling stunts outside the shop while wearing a military uniform.

Indianapolis

Go, Indy Sports!

Indy's fans don't just love their teams—they go crazy over sports at all levels, from the pros to the playgrounds!

INDIANAPOLIS COLTS

Joined the NFL in Baltimore in 1953; moved to Indy in 1984

Cool Stuff: In 2007, led by Peyton Manning, the Colts won the Super Bowl! As of 2022, the Colts have appeared in the playoffs 16 times, won two conference championships, and played in two Super Bowl games, winning for the 2006 season and losing for the 2009 campaign.

Big Names: Peyton Manning, Edgerrin James, Marvin Harrison, Jonathan Taylor

Home: Lucas Oil Stadium

Jonathan Taylor

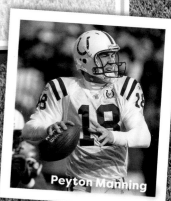

Peyton Manning

FAST FACT

Peyton Manning is so important to the Colts franchise, they built a statue in front of Lucas Oil Stadium. He also continues to have an impact on the city with the Peyton Manning Children's Hospital in Indianapolis.

INDIANA PACERS

Joined the National Basketball Association in 1976

Cool Stuff: The Pacers were an original team when the American Basketball Association (ABA) started in 1967. They went on to win three ABA championships in the 1970s. The Pacers joined the NBA in 1976, but struggled until they drafted Reggie Miller in 1987. He led them to an NBA Finals appearance against the Lakers in 2000. Reggie went on to be an NBA Hall of Famer and one of the greatest 3-point shooters in the game.

Big Names: Reggie Miller, Coach Bobby Leonard, George McGinnis, Mel Daniels

Home: Gainbridge Fieldhouse

FAST FACT

Why Pacers? The people who started the team picked Pacers because of the Indianapolis 500's "pace" car, which starts off the race. It also connects to a type of horseracing called harness racing, which uses horses called . . . pacers.

Reggie Miller

INDIANA FEVER

Joined the WNBA in 2000

Cool Stuff: Just a year after the Fever joined the WNBA, they drafted Tamika Catchings, who became a dominant player. She led the Fever during a 12-year stretch from 2005-2016, when the Fever advanced to the WNBA Finals three times. In 2012, the Fever won the WNBA Championship! It was the first professional basketball title won by an Indianapolis team since 1973.

Big Names: Tamika Catchings, Katie Douglas, Natalie Williams, Kelsey Mitchell

Home: Gainbridge Fieldhouse

Tamika Catchings

Tamika Catchings was a 10-time All Star, five-time Player of the Year, and a four-time Olympic Gold Medalist. She retired in 2016 and was elected to the Naismith Hall of Fame.

INDY ELEVEN SOCCER

Joined the North American Soccer League in 2014 and moved to the USL Championship league in 2018.

Cool Stuff: Indy Eleven played its first game on April 12, 2014. The Indy Eleven name reflects the 11 players on the field of play in addition to paying tribute to the 11th Regiment of Indiana Volunteers, which fought for the Union Army during the Civil War. On the field, Indy Eleven captured its first trophy in 2016 by winning the NASL's Spring Season Championship.

Home: IUPUI—Carroll Stadium

INDY ELEVEN WOMEN

Joined the first USL W League in 2022.

Cool Stuff: Indy Eleven Women went undefeated in its first season, capturing the Great Lakes Division title! They competed in the eight-team USL W League Playoffs, losing in the first round.

Players: Indy Eleven Women are a pre-professional team with former college players and current high school athletes working toward establishing women's pro soccer in Indianapolis.

INDIANAPOLIS INDIANS

A charter member of the minor-league American Association (AA) since 1902, the Indianapolis Indians baseball club has provided over a century of professional baseball in Central Indiana. The team has won 20 league or divisional titles and provided training for several future major league stars and a handful of future Hall-of-Famers.

Former famous Indians include Randy Johnson and Harmon Killebrew. **Home:** Victory Field in White River State Park

Negro League Legacy

Before Black players were allowed to play in the Majors, the Negro Leagues created all-Black teams that played great baseball and drew big crowds. The Indianapolis Clowns and Indianapolis ABCs were a big part of those Negro Leagues. In fact, the first ever Negro National League game took place in Indy in 1920 when the ABCs hosted (and beat!) the Chicago American Giants. Future home run champ Hank Aaron played for the Clowns. One of the best all-around players of all time, Oscar Charleston (right), was born in Indianapolis and played for the ABCs and Clowns.

Indy Sports Stories

The Great One's First Goal

One of the greatest hockey players of all time, Wayne Gretzky, was drafted by the World Hockey Association's Indianapolis Racers. As a 17-year-old in 1978, he scored his first goal in Market Square Arena in Indianapolis. After scoring three goals and recording three assists in eight games for the Racers, Gretzky's career in Indiana was over when he was traded to the Edmonton Oilers of the NHL.

Wayne Gretzky

Olympic Trials

Indy has been the site of great performances in a variety of amateur sports: The Indiana University Natatorium in downtown Indianapolis has hosted 13 individual Olympic Trials. Many swimming and diving world records have been broken at the Natatorium.

INDIANAPOLIS

NASCAR Comes to Indy

The Indy 500 is run with "open-wheel" racing cars. In 1994, another popular racing series began to compete at the Speedway. NASCAR brings its powerful stock cars to the track each summer; since 2021, NASCAR has used the Speedway's twisty road track, not the oval.

College Sports Heaven!

As the home of the headquarters of the NCAA, Indy has also hosted a wide variety of Division I NCAA National Championships, including Men's and Women's NCAA Final Fours. As of 2022 Indianapolis has hosted eight Men's Final Fours. The city also hosted the College Football Playoff Championship Game at Lucas Oil Stadium for the first time in 2022. This was the first time that a college football national championship game was played outside of the South or West.

Indianapolis Motor Speedway

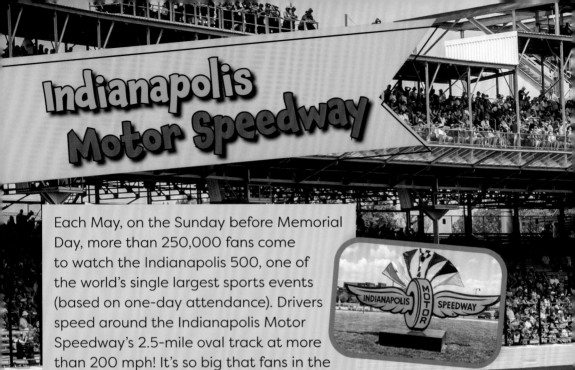

Each May, on the Sunday before Memorial Day, more than 250,000 fans come to watch the Indianapolis 500, one of the world's single largest sports events (based on one-day attendance). Drivers speed around the Indianapolis Motor Speedway's 2.5-mile oval track at more than 200 mph! It's so big that fans in the grandstands can't see all around the track.

The Brickyard

It took 3.2 million bricks to build the first race track at the Indianapolis Motor Speedway when it opened in 1911. The track is not brick anymore, but fans still call it the Brickyard. A yard of bricks does remain at the track's finish line. Winners traditionally kiss the bricks after the race (and after all the cars are off the track!).

FAST FACTS
In 2021, Brazil's Helio Castroneves joined the most exclusive club in auto racing as a four-time winner of the Indy 500 (2001, 2002, 2009, 2021). Castroneves added his name to the list that includes A.J. Foyt, Al Unser, and Rick Mears.

Race teams perform lightning-fast pit stops, changing tires and adding fuel in only a few seconds!

Hinkle Magic

The court may measure the exact same dimensions as other college basketball arenas, but when you walk into Hinkle Fieldhouse, it's different. Maybe it's the echoes of the greatest games with the greatest players in the game of basketball. Or the memories of high school fans who stormed the court in a fit of Hoosier Hysteria after a state tournament win. Or the fact that the nearly 100-year-old court is preserved forever in the classic sports movie, "Hoosiers." When you enter this "Cathedral of Basketball" on the campus of Butler University in Indianapolis, you can feel the Hinkle Magic.

➤ Butler Fieldhouse was constructed in 1928 as the largest basketball arena in the United States—at the time.

➤ The name of the facility was changed in 1966 from Butler Fieldhouse to Hinkle Fieldhouse in honor of Butler's legendary coach and athletic director Paul D. "Tony" Hinkle.

➤ The Fieldhouse was declared a National Historic Landmark in 1987.

Great Start

Larry Bird

At least 70 members of the Naismith Hall of Fame have played or coached on the fieldhouse floor. Two of the best NBA players ever launched their careers as Indiana high school All Stars: Oscar Robertson, star of the Attucks team that won two state titles (page 36), was later "The Big O," one of the best all-around players ever; and Larry Bird, who played at Hinkle as an Indiana All-Star in 1974 and as a member of Indiana State's team in 1977 before going on to NBA superstardom.

The Movie

"Hoosiers" always makes the list of the top sports movies of all time. It was based on a true story. In 1954, tiny Milan High School, with just 161 students, shocked the state by winning the Indiana state title at Hinkle Fieldhouse. They beat the much larger Muncie Central on a last-second shot by Bobby Plump. The 1986 movie was filmed at Hinkle, too.

COLLEGE TOWN

Indianapolis is home to some of the top colleges and universities in the country. Here are a few:

IUPUI

Founded: 1969
Students: 27,690
Popular Majors: Health Professions, Business, Management, Marketing, Engineering
Fast Fact: IUPUI officially stands for Indiana University—Purdue University, Indianapolis. The Indianapolis campuses of IU and Purdue were merged in 1969.

MARIAN UNIVERSITY

Founded: 1851
Students: 2,600
Popular Majors: Registered Nursing; Business Administration and Management; Biology/Biological Sciences; Exercise Science and Kinesiology
Fast Fact: Located just north of the main campus is the Major Taylor Velodrome where the cycling team has won 44 national championships!

UNIVERSITY OF INDIANAPOLIS

Founded: 1902
Students: 5,600
Popular Majors: Registered Nursing, Psychology, Exercise Science and Kinesiology, Banking and Financial Support Services
Fast Facts: UIndy produces more physical therapists, occupational therapists, and clinical psychologists than any other university in the state.

The Atherton Union at Butler University

BUTLER UNIVERSITY

Founded: 1855
Students: 5,000
Popular Majors: Business, Management, Marketing, Communication, Journalism, Education
Fast Fact: Butler came within a ball's bounce of its first NCAA Men's Basketball Championship in 2010 at Lucas Oil Stadium in Indianapolis. The Bulldogs finished as runner-up in their first NCAA Championship appearance.

It's Alive!

Animals in Indianapolis

Indy Wildlife Watch

You don't have to go on a safari to see wild animals in their habitat. The Center for Urban Ecology and Sustainability at Butler University tracks Indianapolis animals four times a year with motion-triggered cameras at city parks, forest preserves, golf courses, agricultural land, schools, and cemeteries. Here are some of the local animals captured on the center's cameras.

Box turtle

Groundhog

Squirrel

Goldfinch

Eagle Creek Reservoir in Indy

Mallard duck

Deer

see iT
AT THE ZOO

The Indianapolis Zoo is a world leader in protecting and caring for animals. Opened in 1964 in Washington Park, the Zoo moved to its current location in White River State Park in 1988. The Indy Zoo celebrates the biodiversity of the planet. More than 200 animal ambassadors live here, which is the only zoo in the country that is a zoo, aquarium, and botanical garden—all in one.

FAST FACT
The largest animals at the zoo female African elephants, who weigh more than 9,500 pounds!

The tallest animal at the zoo is the giraffe. Both giraffes and humans have seven vertebrae in their necks, though a giraffe's vertebrae can each be up to 10 inches long!

The smallest of all the Zoo critters is the honeybee. This insect plays an important role by pollinating many of the plants in the food chain.

Smooth dogfish sharks can change color to blend into their environments. You can take part in saving ocean species like dog sharks by making good choices and buying sustainable seafood.

Amur tigers are one of the world's largest big cats, growing up to 10 feet in length!

A desert in Indiana? At the zoo . . . yes! In the Desert Domes exhibit, a huge glass ceiling protects animals like this bearded lizard from dry regions around the world.

Dolphin Show

The zoo's free Dolphin Presentations feature bottlenose dolphins. Not only will you be amazed by these powerful and intelligent marine mammals, you'll learn more about the bond they share with Zoo staff. Find out how you can make their world a healthier place by avoiding single-use plastics that put dolphins and other sea animals at risk.

Saving Animal Species

Since 2017, the Global Center for Species Survival at the Indianapolis Zoo has worked with conservationists from around the world to protect species and the spaces they call home.

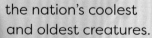

In Indiana, the zoo is helping to increase the population of hellbenders through a breeding program. The hellbender is the largest aquatic salamander in North America and a state-endangered species in Indiana. Baby hellbenders are cared for by the zoo staff, and at Purdue University. They raise hundreds of hellbenders for release into Indiana rivers once they have grown up. They then track the hellbenders to see how they survive. This will help to make sure the river ecosystems are balanced and thriving. The hellbender has been around for 150 million years. To keep waterways clean and healthy, everyone can help conserve the habitat and protect one of the nation's coolest and oldest creatures.

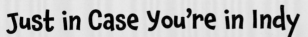

Just in Case You're in Indy

➤ Don't mow grass or graze livestock next to streams; this can lead to erosion and contamination.

➤ Don't pick up or move rocks; this can disturb the habitat for hellbenders.

➤ Dispose of chemicals properly. Don't pour them down storm drains.

➤ Cut the line if you catch a hellbender while fishing.

The salamander known as the hellbender

Spooky Sites

Indy is full of spooky sites you can discover year round. Ghost hunters have lists for the brave who want to go it alone and tours for those who want some company.

The Lincoln Ghost Train

Irvington, a neighborhood in Indianapolis, has haunted tours that are not for the faint of heart. The tour ends with a stop by an old mile marker along the tracks that carried Abraham Lincoln's funeral train back in 1865. The train's been said to reappear, all nine cars intact, draped in black bunting and carrying the late President's body on a raised platform. The attendees, the guards, the train engineers are all there, too—but everyone's a skeleton! It's the most-sighted ghost in America.

Slippery Noodle Inn

The historic buildings that house the Slippery Noodle Inn have been around since 1850, and were part of the Underground Railroad. People report seeing the ghosts of escaping enslaved people, a cowboy, and a caretaker.

Indiana Repertory Theatre

To avoid cold and rainy weather, a former theater director used to jog indoors. But one day, he went out in the fog and was hit by a car—driven by his nephew! Now, on cold and rainy days, witnesses say you can hear the floorboards creak as the director's ghost jogs around the theater.

Crown Hill Cemetery

Crown Hill Cemetery was established in 1863 and has 550 acres. Visitors and employees have spotted the ghost of a woman holding a baby and wandering around the graves, as if she is lost and trying to find her way home. People have also seen American soldiers in uniforms from every American war. Like the woman with the baby, they disappear once they've been spotted.

Central State Hospital

The Indiana Hospital for the Insane turned into the Central State Hospital in 1926. It is said to be haunted by many patients who suffered abuse in the hospital. Witnesses have described shadows, ghosts, women's screams, electrical devices that turn on and off by themselves, unexplained noises, footsteps, and moans.

INDY BY THE NUMBERS

Hoosiers think Indy is No. 1, of course, but here are some stats and numbers to impress you.

14

Indianapolis is the 14th largest city in the US.

8 miles

Length of the Cultural Trail that connects seven districts with attractions, entertainment, and restaurants.

450

Number of major sporting events hosted in the past half century in Indy.

3.2 MILLION
Number of bricks laid to make the track at the Indianapolis Motor Speedway in 1909.

8 minutes
How often the pendulum at the Indiana State Museum knocks down a peg, a process that shows the Earth's rotation.

FAST FACT
Oops! In 1861, Thomas Edison—who became a world-famous inventor—was fired as telegraph operator at Indy's Union Depot for "wasting time on useless experiments."

38 FEET TALL
Height of the statue of Lady Victory atop the Soldiers and Sailors Monument (plus she weighs 20,000 pounds!).

Not Far Away

There's more to explore! While you're visiting Indianapolis, check out these day trips to places nearby.

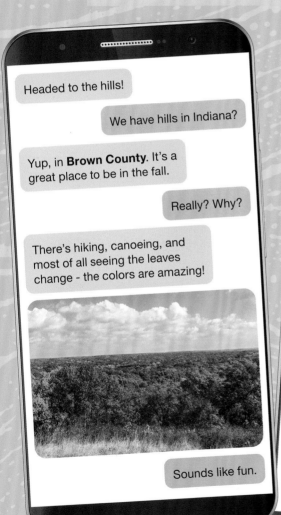

Headed to the hills!

We have hills in Indiana?

Yup, in **Brown County**. It's a great place to be in the fall.

Really? Why?

There's hiking, canoeing, and most of all seeing the leaves change - the colors are amazing!

Sounds like fun.

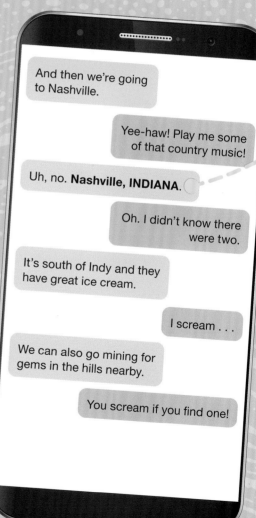

And then we're going to Nashville.

Yee-haw! Play me some of that country music!

Uh, no. **Nashville, INDIANA.**

Oh. I didn't know there were two.

It's south of Indy and they have great ice cream.

I scream . . .

We can also go mining for gems in the hills nearby.

You scream if you find one!

On the road again - to visit Santa Claus!

Wait - you're going to the North Pole?

No that would be crazy - we're going to **Santa Claus, Indiana**. It's only a couple of hours from Indy. It is the only town in the whole world with that name!

Wow! Way to get to the top of the Nice List!

I know. I'll be sending my letter in to the **Santa Claus Post Office** ASAP!

Then I'll make a stop at **Santa's Candy Castle**, for all kinds of candy, fudge, popcorn and 35 kinds of hot chocolate.

Yum!

And Santa Claus (the town) is also the home to **Holiday World**, the oldest theme park in America. It has rides and areas that celebrate the other major holidays!

Merry Happy Day Week Year! 🎅

Hi! Texting from the **Ohio River in Corydon**!

Wait – I've heard that name before . . .

It was Indiana's first state capital. Not only will we see the old capital building, but also the most important tree in Indiana, the **Constitution Elm**.

What makes the tree so special?

It is where the first state legislators wrote Indiana's constitution in 1816. Only the trunk of the tree remains.

Next stop: More shade, but in a different way.

Bigger tree?

Nope, underground! **Squire Boone Caverns**.

Spooky!

The park is named for the brother of famous frontiersman Daniel Boone.

I think I saw an old TV show!

Well, Squire never got to take the zipline ride in the woods nearby that we did! We also found prehistoric fossils in the caves.

We turned the car around and are now heading north to **Fort Wayne**—the second largest city in Indiana!

Never been there - so what's up?

We're going to where Fort Wayne's three rivers meet at **Promenade Park**. Lots to explore there - kayaking, hiking, biking, and even airboat rides!

Sound likes you'll be on the move!

You betcha! There's so much history. It's the site of the Miami people's most important city, Kekionga.

That's going back a while!

Also, the **Kekionga Baseball Grounds** is the site of the first professional baseball game in 1871.

KEKIONGA
BALL GROUNDS
1869 — 1871

Batter up!

And there's more—a **Children's Zoo** and the hands-on **Science Central**.

Who knew the beach was only about 3 hours from Indianapolis?

Where are you - Florida?

Nope, still in Indiana. We're about as far north as you can get and still be in the Hoosier State . . .

Tell me where!

We're at **Indiana Dunes National Park**, on the south shore of Lake Michigan.

It has 15 miles of sandy beach for swimming, boating and fishing. There's so much wildlife here. The dunes are wild!

Dunes????

Dunes are hills of sand that are formed by the wind. I'm taking on the 3 Dune Challenge and will try to climb the three tallest sand dunes at the Indiana Dunes National Park. It's 552 vertical feet! I will be king of the Dune World!

You can do it! 👍

You've heard of waterparks, right?

Splish, splash!

Well, there's one not far from Indy that's not just a park . . . it's a lake!

Get out!

Get in! The water, I mean. **Pine Lake Waterpark** is only open during the summer.

Too cold, otherwise, right?

Brr. But perfect for summer splashing.

They have slides, tubes, and boats to rent.

Look out below!

It's in a beautiful place, too. You zip down tubes to a lake surrounded by trees!

Sounds like a blast!

I know! I went on the slides about a zillion times!

You must be a raisin by now!

Sister Cities Around the World

For more than 25 years, Indy has reached across the globe and expanded the "family." The International Center is a partner of the Indianapolis Sister Cities International program through the Mayor's Office of International and Cultural Affairs. Sister Cities was started in 1956 as a program of the US government. The idea was to connect cities around the world to help people get to know each other. Today, Indianapolis has relationships with nine Sister Cities!

Northamptonshire, United Kingdom
Cologne, Germany
Monza, Italy
Piran, Slovenia
Hangzhou, China
Taipei, Taiwan
Hyderabad, India
Onitsha, Nigeria
Campinas, Brazil

Indianapolis's Sister Cities

Sister Cities in Action

Here are some examples of how the people of Indianapolis are working with and helping their Sister Cities:

Sister Cities Fest: Each year, the Taste the Difference Festival & Sister Cities Fest allows people to travel the world without leaving Indy with food samples and performances by groups representing countries around the world. The proceeds promote Sister Cities cultural exchanges.

Cologne, Germany: Every year since 2010, a firefighter has traveled to a Sister City to participate in a three-week exchange. The firefighters live with host families and work alongside the Sister City firefighters at their stations and are treated as employees.

Taipei, Taiwan celebrates the Dragon Boat Festival. Families and friends get to watch dragon boat races and eat dumplings. There are also dragon boat races in the US and Indy has its own team, Indy SurviveOars, that competes across the nation.

Books

Indiana Bicentennial Commission. *Indiana at 200: A Celebration of the Hoosier State.* Evansville, IN: M.T. Publishing, 2015.

Humphrey, David. *Indianapolis: The City Known as Naptown.* Mount Pleasant, SC: Arcadia Publishing, 2022.

Petry, Ashley. *Indianapolis: An Illustrated Timeline.* St. Louis, MO: Reedy Press, 2021.

Tenuth, Jeffrey. *Indianapolis: A Circle City History.* Mount Pleasant, SC: Arcadia Publishing, 2004.

Web Sites

Indiana Historical Bureau
www.in.gov/history

Visit Indy
https://www.visitindy.com/

Encyclopedia of Indianapolis
https://indyencyclopedia.org/

Eiteljorg Museum
https://eiteljorg.org/for-educators/educator-resources/

Indianapolis Zoo
https://www.indianapoliszoo.com/

Indianapolis Motor Speedway
https://www.indianapolismotorspeedway.com/

Things to Do With Kids in Indianapolis
https://indywithkids.com/

Photo Credits and Thanks

All photos from Dreamstime, iStock, Library of Congress, Shutterstock, or Wikipedia, along with these sources:

AP Photo: John Swart 28B; Darron Cummings 29B; Fred Jewell 40T; The Herald Bulletin 41BR; Brian Spurlock/Icon Sportswire 66main; Brian Henton 71R. Newscom: Darrell Walker/UTHM 61BR; Pat Lovell/Cal Sport Media 62T; Jeffrey Brown/Cal Sport Media 63T; Amy Sanderson/ZUMA Press 65R; Michael Allio/Icon Sportswire 66L, 67R; Zach Bollinger/Icon Sportswire 70 main. NE Indiana Public Radio: 16 (map). US Army Center for Military History: 18 bkgd. National Archives: 18 TR. IUPUI University Library Center for Digital Scholarship: 22 (map). Indiana Humanities/Flikr: 76 (dolphins). Robbins Photography: 34, 35TR, 36B, 37TR, 47BRm 61TR. Doug Kerr/Flickr: 85 (2). Wanderer/Flickr: 86 (elm). Artwork:

Lemonade Pixel; Maps (6-7) by Jessica Nevins.
Cover typography by Swell Type.

Thanks to our pal Nancy Ellwood, Jessica Rothenberg, and the fine folks at Arcadia Children's Books!

INDEX

Thanks for Visiting

INDIANAPOLIS

Come Back Soon!